White Suits in Summer

by Rosary Hartel O'Neill

A Samuel French Acting Edition

New York Hollywood London Toronto

SAMUELFRENCH.COM

Copyright © 2010 by Rosary Hartel O'Neill
ALL RIGHTS RESERVED

CAUTION: Professionals and amateurs are hereby warned that *WHITE SUITS IN SUMMER* is subject to a licensing fee. It is fully protected under the copyright laws of the United States of America, the British Commonwealth, including Canada, and all other countries of the Copyright Union. All rights, including professional, amateur, motion picture, recitation, lecturing, public reading, radio broadcasting, television and the rights of translation into foreign languages are strictly reserved. In its present form the play is dedicated to the reading public only.

The amateur and professional live stage performance rights to *WHITE SUITS IN SUMMER* are controlled exclusively by Samuel French, Inc., and licensing arrangements and performance licenses must be secured well in advance of presentation. PLEASE NOTE that amateur licensing fees are set upon application in accordance with your producing circumstances. When applying for a licensing quotation and a performance license please give us the number of performances intended, dates of production, your seating capacity and admission fee. Licensing fees are payable one week before the opening performance of the play to Samuel French, Inc., at 45 W. 25th Street, New York, NY 10010.

Licensing fee of the required amount must be paid whether the play is presented for charity or gain and whether or not admission is charged.

Professional/Stock licensing fees quoted upon application to Samuel French, Inc.

For all other rights than those stipulated above, apply to: The Marton Agency, 1 Union Square, Suite 815, New York, NY 10003; Info@MartonAgency.com.

Particular emphasis is laid on the question of amateur or professional readings, permission and terms for which must be secured in writing from Samuel French, Inc.

Copying from this book in whole or in part is strictly forbidden by law, and the right of performance is not transferable.

Whenever the play is produced the following notice must appear on all programs, printing and advertising for the play: "Produced by special arrangement with Samuel French, Inc."

Due authorship credit must be given on all programs, printing and advertising for the play.

ISBN 978-0-573-69766-1   Printed in U.S.A.   #25278

No one shall commit or authorize any act or omission by which the copyright of, or the right to copyright, this play may be impaired.

No one shall make any changes in this play for the purpose of production.

Publication of this play does not imply availability for performance. Both amateurs and professionals considering a production are strongly advised in their own interests to apply to Samuel French, Inc., for written permission before starting rehearsals, advertising, or booking a theatre.

No part of this book may be reproduced, stored in a retrieval system, or transmitted in any form, by any means, now known or yet to be invented, including mechanical, electronic, photocopying, recording, videotaping, or otherwise, without the prior written permission of the publisher.

MUSIC USE NOTE

Licensees are solely responsible for obtaining formal written permission from copyright owners to use copyrighted music in the performance of this play and are strongly cautioned to do so. If no such permission is obtained by the licensee, then the licensee must use only original music that the licensee owns and controls. Licensees are solely responsible and liable for all music clearances and shall indemnify the copyright owners of the play and their licensing agent, Samuel French, Inc., against any costs, expenses, losses and liabilities arising from the use of music by licensees.

IMPORTANT BILLING AND CREDIT REQUIREMENTS

All producers of *WHITE SUITS IN SUMMER* must give credit to the Author of the Play in all programs distributed in connection with performances of the Play, and in all instances in which the title of the Play appears for the purposes of advertising, publicizing or otherwise exploiting the Play and/or a production. The name of the Author *must* appear on a separate line on which no other name appears, immediately following the title and *must* appear in size of type not less than fifty percent of the size of the title type.

CHARACTERS

BLAISE SALATICH – A handsome, out-of-work actor, 28.

LUCILLE – His serious wife, an art critic, 38.

SUSANNE DUPRÉ – His ex-lover, a famous painter, 28.

TED CLAPPER – Her frustrated manager, 26.

OFFSTAGE VOICES of priests, nurse, and a cop.

SETTING

A mansion on Exposition Boulevard, New Orleans. We are in a big, finely-proportioned parlor with a high ceiling, Oriental rug, a crystal chandelier. The atmosphere is that of a grand sanctuary, where the landowner can view Audubon Park as a superior. Floor-to-ceiling windows, sometimes used as entrances, open onto a gallery overlooking a wide lawn, which tumbles onto Audubon Park. During the daytime one has the feeling of a semi-tropical park, and at night of an oak garden, which climbs into the stars.

TIME

The present. Sunshine, already hard on the windows, fills the room with a sharp light.

First performed March 1998 as *Exposition Boulevard* Southern Rep Theater, New Orleans.

WHITE SUITS IN SUMMER

ACT ONE

Scene One

(A summer day. Noon. The present. Several suitcases line the stage. **LUCILLE**, *38, runs onstage. She's very healthy with a mass of hair and deep-set hazel eyes. There is a curious blend of country carelessness and intelligence. Her husband,* **BLAISE**, *enters, buttoning his shirt. He is handsome, about 28, but his carriage makes him appear older. He is tall, long-limbed with a wide forehead, thick brown hair, and fine sensitive eyes. He wears conservative dark clothes, obviously expensive, and he wears them well. Harsh sunlight falls over the gallery as* **TED CLAPPER**, *in a rumpled white suit, approaches. He checks back for fear his car will be towed. An effusive businessman, he's in his twenties, but his face looks older.)*

TED. Anybody home? *(Crosses to* **BLAISE***)* Teddy Clapper.

LUCILLE. Who?

TED. New Orleans Country Club? Southern Yacht Club? Now I'm managing Susanne Dupré.

LUCILLE. Susanne Dupré. *(Screams in delight)* Oh my. Oh God. Oh, no.

TED. *(Searches about)* My glasses broke. I've a second pair.

LUCILLE. I'll fix them. You know my husband. *(To herself)* Oh my God. Susanne Dupré.

BLAISE. Can I help you with something?

TED. Mom and I want you to host an exposition of Susanne Dupré.

LUCILLE. *(To* **BLAISE***)* This is the miracle we've been waiting for.

TED. *(Looks out)* They're not giving me a ticket? I double-parked by a fire hydrant, then barged into the curb...

BLAISE. You should move your car.

WHITE SUITS IN SUMMER

TED. Like I said, we're looking for patrons to do an exposition of...

(Phone rings. **TED** *searches for phone, gives up when ringing stops.)*

TED. Mom might phone. I've rough car trips calling her. She fired the night watchman and bought me a phone. My mother is the sweetest, panicked person on earth. I advanced up to escort when Dad departed this world...

LUCILLE. I saw it in the obituaries.

TED. A show on Exposition Boulevard could be an important event. Susanne's a young legend.

LUCILLE. A practitioner of the—

TED. Nobler forms.

LUCILLE. Her show in Berlin left me—

TED. Ecstatic as did her show at the—

LUCILLE and **TED** Guggenheim in New York.

*(***TED***'s cell phone rings. He waves it off.)*

TED. We'll ignore that. All Mom's friends are dying, so it's not great for her. Her two best friends died within weeks. What with her heart surgery and the cataracts...

(Phone stops ringing. He searches for the scrapbook and pictures.)

TED. Mom made a scrapbook of your wedding. She keeps saying, "Why couldn't you've married Lucille?" *(To* **LUCILLE***)* Every boy at Jesuit High School was in love with you.

BLAISE. *(To* **TED***)* Thanks for the gift.

LUCILLE. *(to* **TED***)* Your glasses fixed.

TED. Amazing. *(Phone rings,* **TED** *answers it)* Hello there. *(To* **BLAISE***)* If I

WHITE SUITS IN SUMMER

don't respond instantly, Mom calls the cops. *(Talks into the phone)* Yeah, Mom. I gave Lucille the clippings and the...no. *(To himself)* Where are those grapefruit spoons? *(Checks about; to* **LUCILLE***)* Mom had them replaced. *(To* **BLAISE***)* My family's in fine jewelry and heirlooms. *(Into the phone)* I got them. *(Hangs up)*

LUCILLE. *(Peeking in the box)* Another priceless treasure from Uncle.

TED. Mom says ya'll have the finest art collection.

BLAISE. He gave it to the museum.

(Phone rings, but **TED** *ignores it, looking for an outlet to recharge it.)*

TED. If I'm gone long, she'll find me—hunt me down. My sister came for a month with her kids—wild, exhausting six, seven, and twelve-year-olds. After she left, it required weeks of down time to revive Mother.

LUCILLE. Wouldn't it be wonderful to have kids 'round the house?

TED. Little Lucilles and—

BLAISE. We're not having children yet.

LUCILLE. I didn't mean today.

TED. Where's that outlet?

BLAISE. With Uncle Gene's illness and—

LUCILLE. Blaise's goal is to become a great actor, get fame, start his own production company.

TED. *(Interrupting, to* **BLAISE***)* Say, weren't you and Susanne schoolmates at—?

BLAISE. Berkeley.

TED. Right. I told Susanne a political edge would move her ahead faster. She started her triangle series in Berlin.

*(***BLAISE** *guides him to an outlet.)*

WHITE SUITS IN SUMMER

LUCILLE. Splendid.

TED. I organized this smashing opening at the Mary Boon in New York. She constructed and deconstructed Naughty Marietta and the Casket Girls at the Whitney. *(TED's phone rings)* Mom gets foggy and keeps calling. *(Speaks into the phone)* I'll pick you up for dinner.

(He hangs up. The phone rings again. **TED** *throws up his hands.)*

TED. Each time, it's an earnest pitch—when can I expect you? Mom's got a housekeeper, a chauffeur, and a cook, but she's essentially alone. Eating out and her poodle, "Bootsy," are all that keep her going. Pardon me. *(Picks up the phone and talks to his Mom)* Yes, I gave them the—no, no. I'll do it. More gifts—certificates for silver frames for your wedding portrait and invitation, and for baby rattles, cups, brushes, diaper pins, cutlery, and dishes. All to be engraved later.

LUCILLE. How extravagant.

TED. We've tons of wedding and baby gifts—never bought or returned—and Mom wants you to have them all—in case something... She should never have had heart surgery of that magnitude. *(Into the phone)* Yes. She's got it. Goodbye, Mom. *(Hangs up the phone)* I handle Mom's expenses, the understatement of the year. Time's coming when I'll have to move in—

BLAISE. *(Checks his watch)* Excuse me.

TED. Wait. About the show—

LUCILLE. 'Course we'll sponsor it. We'll use the side gallery.

TED. Excellent.

LUCILLE. Uncle will contribute. I've got great ambitions for **BLAISE.**

TED. Is that a meter maid out there? What?

LUCILLE. Don't leave.

TED. No, I thought you said... Three shapes of them are ticketing my car. Bat women from hell. *(To* **LUCILLE***)* I'll be right back.

WHITE SUITS IN SUMMER

BLAISE. Take your time. I'm going for a smoke. *(Exits)*

(Moments later. **Lucille***, high-strung, turns up a baby-minder, a ritual she deals with continually.)*

(SOUND: **UNCLE GENE***, moaning upstairs.)*

LUCILLE. *(Speaks into the machine)* Nurse? Can't you ease Uncle's pain?

NURSE. *(offstage)* I've got a call in to the doctor.

*(***SUSANNE***, 28, enters quietly with her portfolio and paint box. She is dressed casually in seductive clothes. Hollows shadow her cheeks and her slender neck. There is a quality of nervous tension, the mental strain of an artist who puts unrelieved pressure on herself.)*

SUSANNE. Hi. I'm Susanne Dupré.

LUCILLE. Oh my. Oh my Lord. You're an absolutely brilliant artist. I'm Lucille, Blaise's wife.

SUSANNE. Hello. Ted sent me in.

LUCILLE. Anyone in love with painting admires your work. *(Looks about)* Where's Ted?

SUSANNE. Parking the car. Is this a bad time?

LUCILLE. Sorry—I'm in such a tether.

SUSANNE. I understand. My challenge is to discern reality.

LUCILLE. Ah. To paint things the way they truly are—

SUSANNE. Not through false glasses.

LUCILLE. New Orleans must be quite an interesting study when—

SUSANNE. Viewed as an outsider. *(Stares at her)* You're lovely. *(Overcome with disappointment)* I don't think I can exhibit here. It's too—fussy.

WHITE SUITS IN SUMMER

(SUSANNE looks out, her face hot and sweating. Music floats in from the Cathedral. Something like Isaiah 6: "Here I am, Lord. It is I, Lord? I have heard you calling in the night. I will go, Lord, if you lead me. I will hold your people in my heart.")

LUCILLE. Choir practice from Holy Name Church. I can hear them even better from my classroom at Tulane.

SUSANNE. *(Avoiding* **LUCILLE***'s face)* You teach?

LUCILLE. Art history. At Tulane.

SUSANNE. What a view. The sun sifting through Spanish moss. And the park dancing all around. I feel like I'm being reborn, nourished by Utopia. People would be calmer if they lived in beauty. Marvelous house.

LUCILLE. It's been in my family for generations.

SUSANNE. And will stay there.

LUCILLE. These houses are great 'cause they keep memory alive. *(Moaning through the baby-minder)* My uncle has cancer.

SUSANNE. Sorry.

LUCILLE. I use a baby-minder. It's sad.

SUSANNE. With a certain—

LUCILLE. If you need to buffer entropy, this is a good training ground.

SUSANNE. My presence feels inappropriate.

LUCILLE. I adored your Berlin exhibit. "How the Feminist and the Archetype Intersect."

SUSANNE. What did your husband think?

LUCILLE. Right. You met Blaise.

WHITE SUITS IN SUMMER

SUSANNE. Well?

LUCILLE. He framed my article comparing your painting to Beckett's drama. *(Hands* **SUSANNE** *the article.)*

SUSANNE. "Apocalyptic Isolation." Some title.

LUCILLE. You're a prodigy.

SUSANNE. People get noticed if they do something unusual and live in New York in their twenties.

LUCILLE. You're welcome to stay—

SUSANNE. There is motion here, but again—it's not the house I was hoping for.

LUCILLE. We could paint the walls, redo some lights.

SUSANNE. *(Shaking her head)* No.

LUCILLE. Blaise needs to meet people in the arts.

SUSANNE. It won't work.

LUCILLE. He wants to do leads in film and theater, the whole panoramic portrait.

SUSANNE. Not tiny parts, shards in the mosaic.

LUCILLE. We can create projects for you both from here.

SUSANNE. *(Picks up a large white album)* Your wedding album.

LUCILLE. There's Blaise kissing me at the altar, feeding me cake.

SUSANNE. You're still newlyweds. Love hasn't changed to respect.

*(***SUSANNE** *fidgets with a cigarette.* **TED** *enters.)*

TED. I can't stay. I promised to take Mom to Antoine's.

WHITE SUITS IN SUMMER

LUCILLE. Don't worry. Susanne and I can discuss the exposition.

SUSANNE. If we have one.

TED. Don't mind her. *(Whispers to* **SUSANNE***)* You'll do what I say.

SUSANNE. I don't know. *(To herself)* Change carries consequence.

TED. I'm off.

*(***LUCILLE*** ushers* **TED** *to the door.* **BLAISE** *enters from the park, brushes past* **SUSANNE***, walks to get liquor.)*

BLAISE. Oh, Susanne.

LUCILLE. Right. You knew each other. Kiss me, dear. *(He kisses her)* We're still honeymooning.

BLAISE. Excuse me. *(Leaving)*

LUCILLE. Don't be rude, darling. I need your input on the exposition.

SUSANNE. Maybe you shouldn't have it, just enjoy the park, and—

BLAISE. Can I get you a drink? Every Southern home has a recovery shelf. *(To* **SUSANNE***)* A Bloody Mary?

SUSANNE. Perrier. Might as well drink water with class.

LUCILLE. You'll let us host you?

SUSANNE. Not sure. I feel mostly good about what Ted and I are doing— It's simply a desire for a real home—that the other galleries can't fulfill.

BLAISE. Maybe this need is invalid.

SUSANNE. I think not—

*(***BLAISE*** wipes his forehead, which has broken out in a sweat.* **LUCILLE** *chuckles in the embarrassed silence and passes condiments.)*

WHITE SUITS IN SUMMER

LUCILLE. *(To* **SUSANNE***)* Your use of triangles intrigues me. We must include "Shakti's Heart"—your triangle symbolizing the Hindu Goddess.

BLAISE. It's too Gauguin for me. Actually, that piece depresses me the least.

LUCILLE. Blaise!

BLAISE. *(To* **SUSANNE***)* Weren't you supposed to search out dark, lugubrious triangles?

SUSANNE. The easy expositions are over, and the tough ones just begun.

LUCILLE. Showing here will not be as difficult as you think.

*(***BLAISE** *starts to exit.)*

LUCILLE. You're not leaving? Relax, dear. This is for you.

BLAISE. I like to pace. If I sit, I might miss something.

LUCILLE. *(Clears her throat)* Tell us about your recent work.

SUSANNE. I've been correcting energy-draining behaviors.

LUCILLE. That affect your painting.

SUSANNE. And life.

LUCILLE. Your paintings are sharper.

SUSANNE. Painting is about paying attention in a Buddhist way.

BLAISE. That's hard to do.

SUSANNE. I slip into the skin of people I see—even if it hurts.

LUCILLE. You paint "fruitful blank spaces" which life fills in.

SUSANNE. When I smile...I'm thinking of something enticing.

LUCILLE. You're smiling now? Isn't she, honey?

WHITE SUITS IN SUMMER

SUSANNE. You can use art to heal, to face a part of yourself you hate.

LUCILLE. Go on!

SUSANNE. In my last triangle series, I saw myself in the colors and mended my ways.

LUCILLE. *(To* **SUSANNE***)* How do you know when a painting is finished?

SUSANNE. *(To* **BLAISE***)* When you love it.

(A moan through the baby-minder. A bell rings. **LUCILLE** *rises to leave.)*

LUCILLE. Uncle calls every five minutes.

BLAISE. Nurse is there.

LUCILLE. Yes, but he waits for me. *(To* **BLAISE***)* Darling, get Susanne's press agent, mailing lists. Talk strategy.

SUSANNE. I don't know.

LUCILLE. We'll give you two an outrageous reception: jazz band, oysters etoufées, mint juleps.

SUSANNE. But does the world need another show?

LUCILLE. 'Course. Artists make dreams. *(To* **BLAISE***)* Kiss, kiss, love bug.

*(***LUCILLE*** adjusts the baby-minder and flutters off.* **BLAISE** *gives* **SUSANNE** *a hard look.)*

SUSANNE. Love bug.

BLAISE. When did you move to New Orleans?

SUSANNE. Before your wedding.

BLAISE. You came to our wedding?

WHITE SUITS IN SUMMER

SUSANNE. *(Removes a newspaper notice)* I sat in back of the church. Didn't make the reception.

(SOUND: Doorbell rings.)

MAID. *(offstage)* The prescription. I've got it, Miss Lucille.

(BLAISE turns down the baby-minder.)

SUSANNE. Lucille is, like a mother... You think about California?

BLAISE. I recall lots of dead things. *(Starts to leave)*

SUSANNE. After your wedding, I slept all day. I felt like a part of me was melting—

BLAISE. Now you've seen me and I've seen you.

SUSANNE. Why did you move here? For the?

BLAISE. Restaurants—You can be a starving artist in your teens, but in your twenties you like to dine out occasionally.

SUSANNE. When I started painting, I didn't worry about sales.

BLAISE. As long as you work for your soul, it's great.

SUSANNE. Sometimes I can't—sleep.

BLAISE. You need to—

SUSANNE. I'm not taking pills or fooling around.

(LUCILLE enters with mail to get a bottle of gin.)

LUCILLE. The mail came.

BLAISE. My headshots!

LUCILLE. Why send them? Soon, we'll produce you here. Money's the crucial factor.

WHITE SUITS IN SUMMER

SUSANNE. And talent.

LUCILLE. Persistence. I won't let Blaise fail. *(Pause)* Uncle wants a Ramos Gin Fizz made of orange flower, water, and gin.

BLAISE. I'll get it.

LUCILLE. *(Checks the baby-minder)* You plan which paintings to hang. *(Moaning through the baby-minder; she starts to go)* Everything's an argument with Uncle. Is there any nutritional value in gin?

SUSANNE. *(To* **BLAISE***)* Joy and celebration.

LUCILLE. Mm. I can hardly get one job done when something hits me. *(Kisses him boldly)*

BLAISE. I should help you.

LUCILLE. Give me a kiss, pumpkin. A bear kiss. *(Pause—Exits)*

(A breeze rises. **BLAISE** *gazes at* **SUSANNE** *so the light from the great porch lanterns catches her face with streaks of brightness. Distant thunder. The gallery is blanketed with a golden coppery light. A hymn floats from the Cathedral, like "On Eagle's Wings." "And he will raise you up on eagle's wings. And hold you in the palm of his hand.")*

SUSANNE. *(Sings)* "And he will raise you up. And he will raise you up. And he will raise you up...on the last day." I love rain on an unexpected day. Every pore opens to the wind.

BLAISE. Nice.

SUSANNE. That's what I remember about New Orleans. The music—and the rain.

BLAISE. I don't have time for this.

*(**SOUND**: Thunder.)*

WHITE SUITS IN SUMMER

SUSANNE. There's a sense of romance about the rain. The sun is around us, but the rain is within us. *(Removes her sketchbook, draws)* When I got here, the rain seized me. Mind if I draw you?

(She moves closer, drawing him. Footsteps inside. **BLAISE** *calls out.)*

BLAISE. Who's there?

SUSANNE. I'm putting you in a triangle—

BLAISE. Lucille? *(Picks up a book.)*

SUSANNE. Using weightlessness to let your image soar.

BLAISE. Five minutes is all.

SUSANNE. You've a wonderful body.

(With a flickering smile, **BLAISE** *clutches his book like a Bible.)*

BLAISE. I read one self-help book a week—

SUSANNE. Dressed or undressed—

BLAISE. The Greatest Salesman Alive, takes a year to finish 'cause it's—

SUSANNE. Self-hypnosis.

BLAISE. You read one chapter three times a day for a month.

SUSANNE. What contacts do you have here?

BLAISE. None. I'm competitive with people.

SUSANNE. Hold that pose.

BLAISE. I forget how I'm supposed to behave.

*(***BLAISE** *gives* **SUSANNE** *a hard, silencing look.)*

SUSANNE. When I saw you in "Hamlet", you defined the word, star.

WHITE SUITS IN SUMMER

(She takes out his picture as Hamlet. **LUCILLE** *hurries onstage.)*

LUCILLE. We've lovely watercress sandwiches and crab soup. Give me a kiss. *(***LUCILLE** *kisses him)* Oh Lord. She's painting here.

BLAISE. Stay and watch.

LUCILLE. Ooh. Uncle won't eat 'less I join him.

BLAISE. *(To* **LUCILLE***)* I'm tired. Let's go nap.

SUSANNE. I should let you two alone.

LUCILLE. Don't be silly. Uncle cries out for attention. His paper is damp. His milk is warm. There's dust on the floor. The new maid is lazy. She barely came in the month we were gone. Then I've got to prepare the shopping list.

BLAISE. Let me help you.

LUCILLE. No. Sit for **SUSANNE.** You know how Uncle treats the maid when I'm not there.

*(***LUCILLE** *buzzes off.* **BLAISE** *follows uneasily, stands in the doorway as the night turns black.* **SUSANNE** *toys with a palette knife. Seeing it,* **BLAISE** *trembles.* **SUSANNE** *speaks maliciously.)*

SUSANNE. You've broken out in a sweat.

BLAISE. New Orleans is melting me.

SUSANNE. How long have you been unemployed? Eight months?

BLAISE. Warm.

SUSANNE. Nine?

BLAISE. Warmer.

SUSANNE. A year? Two?

WHITE SUITS IN SUMMER

BLAISE. "Regret not the glitter of any lost day." Tennessee Williams.

SUSANNE. What happened in Hollywood?

BLAISE. Nothing.

SUSANNE. You told Lucille you'd talk—

BLAISE. I thought I'd make a bundle.

SUSANNE. Doing what?

BLAISE. Selling chunks of my soul at varying intervals.

SUSANNE. Did you?

BLAISE. I auditioned weekly for months.

SUSANNE. That's a lot of no's.

BLAISE. I was holding on for the word, yes—

SUSANNE. *(Slyly)* To lose yourself in the play?

BLAISE. Right.

SUSANNE. You went to interviews with producers?

BLAISE. Yes.

SUSANNE. Casting directors?

BLAISE. So.

SUSANNE. Ah, Blaise Salatich. You've played all these parts blah-blah-blah.

BLAISE. Exactly.

SUSANNE. Finally, a director of a major picture hires you and he gets fired!

BLAISE. Who told you that?

WHITE SUITS IN SUMMER

SUSANNE. Did you go back to the old ways?

BLAISE. No.

SUSANNE. Numbing yourself with—?

BLAISE. No. I wanted to, by God.

SUSANNE. But you didn't.

BLAISE. I kept busy, worked out. Ran.

(He feels for a cigarette. She takes it out for him.)

SUSANNE. You didn't slip once after so many months?

BLAISE. Never.

SUSANNE. So you auditioned for special parts.

BLAISE. Right.

SUSANNE. You were a hand model? A parts model? What?

BLAISE. Soft porn is what they call it. So.

SUSANNE. What happened on your last audition?

BLAISE. Producer arrives in this enormous barrel-like hat.

SUSANNE. He asked you to his hotel room.

BLAISE. Devouring pistachio nuts, telling me his tale of woe.

(She hands him a drink.)

BLAISE. Asks me to sit on the bed and unbutton my shirt... This can't be happening, I thought. I was anxious, but it was a lead. "I'd like to cast you," he said. So, I took off my shirt. He stared till my ears got hot. This can't be happening, I thought. He made me lie on the bed. Then he undid my belt *(cont.)*

WHITE SUITS IN SUMMER

and unzipped my pants. This can't be happening. I backed off. There was this screaming, this hotness. He came at me with a knife. Blood everywhere, drenching his shirt, pants, the floor. Looked like he was coming at himself with the knife.

SUSANNE. He died.

BLAISE. I'm trashed in California.

(SUSANNE adds ice to his drink.)

(SOUND: A song like, "Here I am, Lord" is heard from the church.)

LUCILLE. *(Entering)* Uncle wants ice chips for his drink. Your sketch is rapturous. *(Looking at SUSANNE's drawing)*

BLAISE. *(to LUCILLE)* Stay, sweetheart.

LUCILLE. Did Susanne agree to—

SUSANNE. I do!

LUCILLE. Glorious.

(LUCILLE exits.)

SUSANNE. You have an agent here?

BLAISE. She calls herself one. The only help I ever got was from other artists. They taught me how to face guerilla warfare, to be outspoken, aggressive.

SUSANNE. You can't be an artist unless you plunge ahead. Courage brings peace. Dream big. Fight back. Nirvana awaits. When you march forward, you stand up for the weak, the old, the silenced poets of the world.

SOUND: A car horn toots.

*(SUSANNE starts, and crosses to **BLAISE**.)*

SUSANNE. I have to go. Ted gets impatient.

WHITE SUITS IN SUMMER

BLAISE. I've missed you.

(BLAISE smiles sadly. The car toots again. **SUSANNE** *hurries out.* **LUCILLE** *enters with a folder.)*

LUCILLE. Good news. Uncle's financing the exposition.

BLAISE. *(Sarcastically)* Victory is ours.

LUCILLE. Ours? Did you drink all this gin?

BLAISE. It's a negotiable indulgence. *(Hands her an envelope)*

LUCILLE. Oh dear.

BLAISE. Why does Uncle send us business letters? You talk all day.

LUCILLE. He's a Soniat. Soon as they have an opinion, it becomes a legal document.

BLAISE. Throw it away.

LUCILLE. Wait, it's a lien on this house. He didn't mention—

BLAISE. He was annoyed, you said—

LUCILLE. With your career and our stay abroad.

BLAISE. But he gave us the house.

LUCILLE. Before he did—he took out a mortgage—

BLAISE. "You don't have to be rich," he said, "when your relatives are rich."

LUCILLE. To pay some of his insurance.

SOUND: Doorbell rings.

NURSE. *(offstage)* Good evening.

MALE VOICE #1. *(offstage)* Patient's sleeping.

WHITE SUITS IN SUMMER

LUCILLE. Dominicans slinking about...badmouthing you to Uncle.

(**LUCILLE** *fixes the baby-minder.*)

MALE VOICE #2. *(offstage)* We brought pictures of the baptistery.

LUCILLE. They snuck this folder by his food tray.

(**LUCILLE** *hands a folder to* **BLAISE.**)

BLAISE. A last will and testament—

LUCILLE. They're promising Uncle Heaven.

BLAISE. He believes these hypocrites.

LUCILLE. He keeps asking for you.

BLAISE. You swore when I said he could live upstairs—

LUCILLE. Would it hurt to have a conversation?

BLAISE. I'm not going to be two-faced.

LUCILLE. Uncle's slipping.

BLAISE. Live in tight-assed denial.

LUCILLE. He says you married me for money, that acting is a profession for—

BLAISE. For parasites? He thinks if I can't get a TV show, I should quit. Everyone wants to see a play for nothing. They expect you to rehearse on your own time, at midnight, when you're depleted, or at 4:00 a.m. before you go to your real job. Find some way an institution can make money off you. Then we have crappy actors, working for free and alienating a dwindling public.

LUCILLE. Can't you say you're also interested in sales?

BLAISE. I'm not getting in that pot. The last man who got in there got eaten.

WHITE SUITS IN SUMMER

(Laughs, but she doesn't join in. His phone rings. He doesn't answer.)

LUCILLE. Uncle thinks you're narcissistic. Well, you do, do for yourself.

BLAISE. What in God's name are you talking about!

LUCILLE. I'm just asking you to visit.

BLAISE. He doesn't respect me.

LUCILLE. You know he...he's...sick. That's why he's irritable, and can't be with you more than five minutes. I love him. I remember how he was when I was a little girl. I can't think of life without— He's not himself, now he's dying.

BLAISE. Are we sure? God!

LUCILLE. The doctor phoned about the living will. Lord, I can't take it. Poke your head in the door.

*(She exits. **BLAISE** gazes after her, breathes deeply. We hear wind from a summer rainstorm, sweeping over the park. He picks up the book, and goes inside. Lights fade.)*

WHITE SUITS IN SUMMER

Scene Two

(The gallery gleams with wetness from a rain. Pink, purple, and blue colors shadow the decor. Dance-hall music plays from the stereo. **BLAISE** *is rehearsing a dance sequence for an audition and talking on the phone.* **SUSANNE** *appears, dressed in an exotic gown. He hangs up.)*

BLAISE. My wife's not home. *(She smiles)* Don't you have an opening?

(He wipes his face, swallows water. **SUSANNE** *strolls over and drinks from his glass.)*

SUSANNE. How are you newlyweds making out?

BLAISE. *(Walks out on the veranda)* Most of the guys I grew up with are still here. Sundays you'll see them running behind baby carriages in the park. Weekdays the wives race-walk and—

SUSANNE. Recount their husbands' infidelities?

BLAISE. *(Observes her with a flickering smile)* My therapy is not to pursue a sexy woman one day at a time, and to spend time with other recovering husbands and not talk about it. Ha.

(He resumes practicing a step. She watches him, her eyes moist.)

SUSANNE. Your hair's fallen over your face. Let me get it.

BLAISE. Don't. Moses came from the mountain and said, "I bear good news and bad news. The good news is I got him down to ten. The bad news is adultery is still in."

SUSANNE. That's in the Far East. If you accept a second-rate provincial marriage in the South, it's a sort of burial.

SOUND: Dance music swells from the stereo.

SUSANNE. Dance with me. Please. The assumption we'll start with is we're not finished.

BLAISE. My wife will be here—

WHITE SUITS IN SUMMER

SUSANNE. Let me enjoy you for a moment—arm's length at a safe distance.

(Her eyes dart up and down his body. She lifts his arms, laughing, stretches them around her, her head near his. She cradles his face. He freezes momentarily, like a deer sensing hunters.)

BLAISE. Shame upon you, Susanne.

SUSANNE. Undo that button.

BLAISE. Remove your hand.

SUSANNE. I love this shirt. Before you, I knew a kiss was something you did with your mouth, but I didn't know what it was.

BLAISE. Stop.

SUSANNE. Lucille couldn't be a good lay—her housecoat is so aesthetically offensive.

BLAISE. Quiet!

SUSANNE. Don't walk away. If you're going to say something, say it to my face.

BLAISE. I've changed.

SUSANNE. You haven't.

BLAISE. I don't require madness, any serious addiction.

SUSANNE. I've been dreaming of you—

BLAISE. The best way to remember something is to forget it.

SUSANNE. You're teasing me.

BLAISE. You know me better.

SUSANNE. I know how you felt me in the dark. I saw your face when you walked down the aisle. You loved me then and you do now.

WHITE SUITS IN SUMMER

BLAISE. That's a strange thing to say—

SUSANNE. I've dreamt of you since you married. I have a sixth sense and your thoughts have flown to me.

BLAISE. Get away.

SUSANNE. I can't wait for dreaming. Now you tell me to tear your memory from my eyes? I can't.

LIGHTS: The veranda lights blink on.

(Suddenly **SUSANNE** *is all nerves and sobs. She buries her head in his shoulder.)*

BLAISE. Shh, go over there.

SUSANNE. Terrible night. Dark, moon yellow and slippery.

*(***LUCILLE** *pounds on the door.)*

LUCILLE. *(offstage)* Blaise! Honey? Help me with these bags!

*(***SUSANNE** *rushes off.* **LUCILLE** *stumbles in, puts down the laundry.)*

BLAISE. That was Susanne. Inviting us for champagne after her show.

LUCILLE. I don't think I can make it.

BLAISE. You look exhausted.

LUCILLE. Uncle's no use for these clothes since he's never—

BLAISE. *(Rubbing her shoulders)* Don't exaggerate.

LUCILLE. Getting out of bed. Still he insists I run by the cleaners...Uncle wants me to pick out his burial suit and store it in a plastic box.

BLAISE. Close your eyes.

WHITE SUITS IN SUMMER

LUCILLE. All his shirts are yellowed—

BLAISE. Wearing you out with errands—

LUCILLE. He demands we fire Nurse.

BLAISE. When he could hire a driver. Has he mentioned the mortgage?

LUCILLE. He makes me read him the headlines, check his stocks.

BLAISE. Explain why we're paying off his personal loan.

LUCILLE. I can't bring the subject up.

BLAISE. You shouldn't have to.

LUCILLE. We'll have to economize while I get him to replenish my accounts. It's scary watching him fail. He gets mad when I say you're unemployed. And when I say Aunt's dead, he screams, "Nobody told me."

BLAISE. His body is shutting down, for God's sake.

LUCILLE. I know he's dying. Lord, I saw the diapers. Go see him.

BLAISE. I can't tell him what he wants to hear.

LUCILLE. He'll be ruthless if you don't comply.

BLAISE. Here's money for the note.

LUCILLE. You pawned your wedding ring? You said you would never!

BLAISE. I'll get it back... Summer stock theaters are auditioning. I've been getting calls.

LUCILLE. You promised we could live here. I can't go off to God knows where. Leave Uncle. Don't be selfish. Next spring is time enough to start all that.

*(***BLAISE*** storms out.* **LUCILLE** *follows.)*

WHITE SUITS IN SUMMER

(The coach lights on the gallery cast a weird glow. **SUSANNE** *returns, disheveled.* **TED**, *in a smart white suit, follows, calling* **SUSANNE**.*)*

TED. Some Latino festival's in the Quarter. I could barely get uptown.

SUSANNE. We don't need the obligatory traffic update.

TED. You look like a leftover from Saturday night. Fix up.

SUSANNE. I'm dressed.

TED. You been drinking again?

SUSANNE. I deal with sponsors best when I'm manic.

TED. I leave you, and you have to get drunk. Sixteen hundred is a lot to sink into a one-time dress.

SUSANNE. I'm trying to figure out—

TED. Comb your hair.

SUSANNE. If I've ever made a fool of myself—

TED. Change that lipstick.

SUSANNE. With these people in the past.

TED. Here's your makeup and purse.

SUSANNE. I'm not carrying this "going to the dance" bag.

TED. Stuart's coming. You needn't cultivate him if he's cold. *(***TED***'s cell phone rings)* But whatever's nice about him, I want you to find it. He never risks sweating. Soon as May ends, he's off to Newport.

*(***SUSANNE*** exits.)*

TED. *(Answers phone)* Ma. I know about the festival. Don't mention that horror again. Susanne goes out of her way to make things difficult...she's not a nymphomaniac.

WHITE SUITS IN SUMMER

(Hangs up, paces; we hear a crash offstage)
TED. Susanne!

SUSANNE. *(offstage)* I'm okay.

TED. *(Calls to* **SUSANNE***)* Hurry up. It's your big show!

*(***BLAISE** *enters in a white jacket with drinks.* **TED** *confronts him.)*

TED. It might be bearable if someone wasn't screwing up her mind. Mother heard you were... I'm beginning to understand those red-eye bus trips. The nights Susanne would cry all the way till morning.

BLAISE. Have a martini.

TED. *(Slaps it off)* What! No! I don't want a shitty drink. I helped her break through her perfectionism... I got her to paint even when she was drinking and walking the floor... And she would still be painting if...

*(***LUCILLE** *enters, dressed in a long gown and carrying a soup tureen.)*

LUCILLE. Turtle soup from the country club.

BLAISE. We're famished.

LUCILLE. Oh Lord. I'm so thrilled about seeing Susanne's show with Susanne.

TED. Y'all go eat. *(Calls)* Susanne! Soup's hot. *(To* **LUCILLE***)* That's what I've been missing—

LUCILLE. Indulgence.

*(***SUSANNE** *enters.* **BLAISE** *looks at her with entrancement.* **TED** *inspects her to make sure she's dressed properly.)*

SUSANNE. I can't eat. Thinking of those turtles without their shells—

BLAISE. You look like you just arrived from New York.

TED. Is that's a compliment?

WHITE SUITS IN SUMMER

SUSANNE. I like to dress up fancy. Leave the Poor Clare nun for the designer dress. *(To* **BLAISE***)* Ted's my motivation.

BLAISE. I wouldn't have thought you needed motivation.

SUSANNE. You've an air of heightened Edwardian elegance.

BLAISE. It's my look.

SUSANNE. Well, it's working.

TED. Honey, put this napkin on. Last time you spilled—

SUSANNE. I'm not wearing a bib.

BLAISE. Please.

SUSANNE. *(To* **BLAISE***)* You must be thirsty?

BLAISE. Especially for a good sherry.

*(***BLAISE** *pours sherry in his soup.)*

TED. Water for me.

SUSANNE. I'll have a drink of water with my two friends.

TED. You only have two friends?

BLAISE. Some people don't have any.

SUSANNE. Blaise likes my humor when I'm half-crazed with exhaustion.

BLAISE. Ted. You needn't have worried about Susanne's drinking.

*(***SUSANNE** *drops her eyes onto the sherry as if she'll drink it, but she only sniffs it with distaste.)*

SUSANNE. I can't believe you didn't trust me.

TED. Well, your mind was wandering, and you were brushing your teeth a lot.

WHITE SUITS IN SUMMER

SUSANNE. You imagined I...

TED. Was taking these big slugs before I could get to you.

SUSANNE. I'm going for a walk. Give me my cape.

TED. I'll accompany you.

SUSANNE. I don't need a Mother. I'm about to scream—

TED. You can't go in the park. All dolled up with that jewelry.

SUSANNE. Don't touch me.

TED. Someone will kill you. Leave your purse.

LUCILLE. Your show's in an hour!

(SUSANNE *leaves,* **BLAISE** *picks up a cigarette, follows her. Uneasy,* **LUCILLE** *arranges the table, watching* **TED**, *who eats nervously and glances out at the two.*)

LUCILLE. Pearl-handled spoons, smooth from years of eating pleasure. How could one be grumpy with such a spoon?

TED. I couldn't.

LUCILLE. My aunt had a service for sixty in this pattern. See?

TED. An acorn's chiseled at the neck.

LUCILLE. She used to count silver after every party...demitasse teaspoons, tablespoons, soup spoons, serving spoons, grapefruit spoons... You're not listening.

TED. I am. I'm just—of course I hear you.

LUCILLE. My aunt had a special drawer for her spoons...she took...

TED. Let me help. You shouldn't have to pick up alone.

WHITE SUITS IN SUMMER

***(LIGHT**: Lights fade.)*

WHITE SUITS IN SUMMER

Scene Three

(7:00 the next morning. Steamy hot. The sun bathes the scene in gold light, intensified by the dampness. **BLAISE**, *in a crumpled white jacket, has been fitfully dozing. Looks at his watch. Grabs a journal, pen, writes.)*

BLAISE. I must be vigilant. Stay honest. *(Writes some more)* Better to hammer stone in a quarry like Howard Roark than to sell my soul to the parasites. *(Phone rings,* **BLAISE** *answers it)* Hello...You want to buy a...No. Susanne has not come back.

*(***BLAISE** *hangs up.* **TED** *rushes in, his suit rumpled.)*

TED. Is that...Susanne?

BLAISE. The phone is a terrible invention that allows people to enter your home without being invited. Your mother.

TED. How could Susanne run off?

BLAISE. I phoned the hospitals.

TED. She's a manic-depressive. Takes four pills a day.

BLAISE. I can't spend my day worrying.

TED. I'm not sure you worry about anyone but yourself... Susanne used to be an addict, smoking pot, sniffing coke; she was an alcoholic...

BLAISE. Coffee?

TED. I never drink coffee in the morning. It keeps me awake.

*(***BLAISE** *pours two jiggers. Hands one to* ***TED.****)*

TED. I've no control over her.

BLAISE. You've more control than anyone else.

TED. I think it's going to come to me—how to deal with her—if I keep running my mouth. God knows what it's doing to my system. I'll probably give birth to six

WHITE SUITS IN SUMMER

ulcers. *(Phone rings,* **TED** *answers it)* Hello, Ma. No, she's not back yet... No one's called. I'm not rude... Look, I can't talk. I said good-bye. Mom. *(Pretends he's talking to someone else)* I'm coming. *(Speaks into the phone)* I'll call you. *(Hangs up the phone, picks up* **BLAISE***'s journal)* What's this? Private concerns—

BLAISE. *(Grabs the book)* How bad off was she?

TED. The others stopped drinking about eleven. They were drunk, and didn't want to get drunker. *(Checks his watch)* At one, she took her paintings and disappeared.

BLAISE. You can't handcuff yourself to her.

TED. Her life's blood's in that show, and the assassins are sharpening their knives.

BLAISE. I told her if you're going to invite critics, at least have ones who like you.

SOUND: Cell phone rings.

(Ted answers and speaks into it.)

TED. Mom?... I can't talk. No. I can barely hear you... God, what! I'll call back when I get privacy.

(Ted hangs up, exits. **BLAISE** *crosses to the liquor tray, pours bourbon in his coffee. Picks up a cigarette and walks to the gallery, returns and sits by the phone.* **LUCILLE** *arrives, lugging a portfolio. She switches up the baby-minder. We hear a moaning. She turns, her eyes strange, unblinking, taking in* **BLAISE***.)*

LUCILLE. After church, the Holy Spirit inspired me. I drove by the Quarter. You won't believe it...I found Susanne's paintings.

BLAISE. Where?

LUCILLE. Literally on the pavement. The manager said Susanne drank herself into a stupor. He took her incapacitated body out of the bar— *(Lifts paintings)* Look. It's her new triangle series.

WHITE SUITS IN SUMMER

(Uncle moans through the baby-minder. **LUCILLE** *looks up, nervous.* **BLAISE** *puts away the portfolio.)*

BLAISE. I'll take these till later.

NURSE. *(offstage)* It's Nurse. Your uncle's having difficulty breathing. I've called an ambulance.

LUCILLE. Oh God. We can't take him to...

NURSE. *(offstage)* Doctor wants him at the hospital.

LUCILLE. Yesterday he was his impish self. *(Laughs nervously)*

NURSE. *(offstage)* He needs you.

LUCILLE. Where's the holy water? And those relics? I keep thinking if he doesn't go to the hospital, he won't die.

*(***LUCILLE*** exits. Squad car sirens blare.* **BLAISE** *hides the paintings. Flashing lights brighten the gallery. There are scrambling sounds outside, car doors slamming.)*

LUCILLE. *(offstage)* What's that?

BLAISE. A police car.

TED. *(Rushing on)* Was I parked in the wrong zone?

*(***SUSANNE*** traipses in, barefoot, with a rumpled newspaper. Her sequined gown is ripped, her hair messed, her eyes glazed. A cape flung over her keeps falling off.)*

COP'S VOICE. *(offstage)* I'm on a twenty-one flag-down with a nineteen. Took her from the VCD to the Second District.

TED. Who was that?

SUSANNE. The city's most prominent policeman. He teaches sailing at the Southern Yacht Club, where he and his family are members. He doesn't put the people he arrests in the police report; they go on the society page.

WHITE SUITS IN SUMMER

TED. Let me get that cape. There's blood in your hair. A cut on your shoulder.

SUSANNE. I always dress wrong.

TED. *(Exiting)* I'll get something to wash you up.

SUSANNE. *(Looks at her corsage)* My flowers are wilted. They were happy earlier, but now they're grieving. Throw them out. *(Yanks off petals and mumbles)* He loves me. He loves me not. He loves me—

BLAISE. Not.

SUSANNE. I don't listen to the words.

BLAISE. I'd like to start my day not talking to you. So the first hours aren't spoilt-

SUSANNE. Sorry. I was trying to be successful; partially to impress you and partially to get your sympathy if that didn't work out. I'm going to ask for what I want, as soon as I figure out what that is—

BLAISE. Cigarette, maybe?

(BLAISE passes one to her. She bursts out sobbing.)

SUSANNE. The trouble with past relationships is they're endless.

BLAISE. Have a smoke?

SUSANNE. I'm holding out for as long as I can. I've stopped, but I don't know if I've quit. *(Laughs, holds her forehead)* Oh, my head.

BLAISE. Let me close these blinds. You don't have to kill yourself. Sleep.

(SOUND: Choir practice from Holy Name Church resounds a hymn like, "I danced in the morning when the world was begun, And I danced in the moon and the stars and the sun. And I came down from heaven and I danced on earth at Bethlehem.")

(She pulls him down on her. They kiss.)

WHITE SUITS IN SUMMER

End of Act One

WHITE SUITS IN SUMMER

ACT ONE

Scene One

(Parlor. **BLAISE** *leans over and kisses* **SUSANNE***, who looks bruised and delicate.* **TED** *enters. He and* **BLAISE** *wear the same crumpled white suits from before.)*

TED. *(To* **BLAISE***)* You used to be lovers.

BLAISE. Says who?

TED. Mother. She did some research. You're tormenting Susanne.

BLAISE. Please!

TED. She can't be creative around you.

SUSANNE. It's okay, Ted.

TED. No, it's not. You were on the verge of greatness—. Now look at you. Walking around comatose. Remembering Blaise's comments, and saying your talent's lost. What's he doing to you?

BLAISE. Have you forgotten I'm married?

TED. I haven't forgotten your lovely wife, but evidently you have. *(Yelling offstage)* WHY DON'T YOU GO TO YOUR WIFE?

BLAISE. Fine.

(Exits. **TED** *goes to the bar, seizes a drink.)*

TED. What happened after you left the party?

SUSANNE. I was drinking in the Napoleon House. I think I was drinking there. I hope I was—there. Ha!

TED. And afterwards?

WHITE SUITS IN SUMMER

SUSANNE. They say I got in a brawl over some Mardi Gras beads, was beat up. There's this huge gash on my shoulder.

TED. What do you remember?

SUSANNE. Not much. I forgot my shoes.

TED. *(Alarmed)* And your paintings?

SUSANNE. I left them...someplace.

TED. Try to recall where.

SUSANNE. Wait...wait...no...nothing. It's over.

TED. Think now.

SUSANNE. The exposition of Susanne Dupré.

TED. Think hard!

SUSANNE. I don't want to—

TED. Why not?

SUSANNE. These aren't my people in the stiff suits and straight chairs.

TED. WHAT SHOULD I MAKE OF THAT CRACK?

SUSANNE. I thought I'd be happy seeing the...applause.

TED. AND YOU WERE!

SUSANNE. How do I hold on to reality? When can I paint?

TED. Let's find the paintings you lost.

SUSANNE. People say talk about yourself, paint later.

TED. I come from a line of Southerners with modest talent.

WHITE SUITS IN SUMMER

SUSANNE. Oh, please!

TED. I wanted to lift you to world class. You've ten shows this month.

SUSANNE. Cancel them.

TED. You've spent the money. You know the work it took to get those? You're going to drop your schedule? Become a floating artist? Why are you the talk of the art scene? Because you've got me pushing you and panting ten steps behind. God. I should have seen the narcissist you are. Always sending me to do one more thing. I'm disgusted. You want to cancel things? Fine. Where's my coat? Remember the revenue of the art business is the same as sausage.

SUSANNE. *(Calls after)* You don't mind what mediocrity I paint, long as you can sell it.

(TED exits. Doorbell rings. Offstage, we hear NURSE answer and priests enter, whispering and fawning.)

(BLAISE enters. Susanne undoes her blouse, exposing a shoulder wound. There is a startling change in BLAISE's manner. He crosses cautiously to her.)

SUSANNE. Would you...fix this...bandage?

BLAISE. You're scary.

SUSANNE. It looks more theatrical than it is. *(Gestures to the newspaper)* You saw the review in the Times?

BLAISE. You remember that book that says you have to pass through stages to evolve? That critic hasn't passed through stage one.

SUSANNE. Take a look.

(She hands him the paper. BLAISE turns on a silk lamp and reads. A flicker of light, narrow and intense, streams down. Church bells chime seven o'clock.)

BLAISE. Nasty.

SUSANNE. I'm so embarrassed.

WHITE SUITS IN SUMMER

BLAISE. Does he have some vendetta against you?

SUSANNE. I have to stop reading these notices.

BLAISE. "The event was very organized," he says. "Thank God. I'd hate to think it meant something."

SUSANNE. My flesh crawls when I hear that voice coming through the pages.

BLAISE. Never listen to those who demean your gift.

SUSANNE. I felt the slaughter coming—

BLAISE. Their motive is envy always.

SUSANNE. It happens every now and then, but I was hoping for then and not now.

BLAISE. Art's a bleak world—

SUSANNE. I shouldn't let it hurt me.

BLAISE. You're human—

SUSANNE. Chaotic moments come but... Sometimes I just feel wounded.

BLAISE. Everyone has a broken heart. Everyone has suffered or will suffer incredible loss. Don't budge. Don't bow. You don't have to hide and lick your wounds like the youthful Cezanne.

SUSANNE. I hated those paintings. I had sessions with Ted, went away—

BLAISE. Monet refused to show his water lilies—

SUSANNE. And came back with something that'd deteriorated.

BLAISE. Faberge told his artists to dream of golden castles.

SUSANNE. I've been dreaming about you—of how hard these months have been—

WHITE SUITS IN SUMMER

BLAISE. *(His voice drops)* They were tough on everybody.

SUSANNE. Lucille's made a big splash in the papers.

(BLAISE takes out a cigarette, tosses it aside.)

BLAISE. You're not going to force me to do something, not in my best interest—

SUSANNE. You like it with her?

BLAISE. Lucille is kind, reliable. She won't run off with—

SUSANNE. You've anesthetized yourself?

BLAISE. I'm going to be working in my own theater business.

SUSANNE. Where?

BLAISE. Summer stock theaters are starting up.

SUSANNE. There's none here.

BLAISE. We'll open one. I'll do it slower than you'd want me to. Time line, one to two years to get running. In my later years I'd like to be back in New York.

SUSANNE. Where do we fit...together?

BLAISE. You're doing what you need to for your career, and you're making progress.

SUSANNE. Not true.

SOUND: The morning angelus chimes from Holy Name Church. Sunlight glows over the park.

BLAISE. I wish you well. I do, I mean it.

SUSANNE. You can't expect me to hang around—watching you two—

BLAISE. It's kind of a *marriage blanc*—

WHITE SUITS IN SUMMER

SUSANNE. Night after night—

BLAISE. A sexless marriage— *(Retrieves the paintings and turns to her with pleading eyes)* Lucille found your sketches—slightly damaged.

SUSANNE. I don't care about the paintings, strangely—

BLAISE. You can repair them. Throw yourself into—

SUSANNE. Burn them. I don't want to paint now.

BLAISE. 'Course you do.

SUSANNE. Are you keeping them to torture me?

BLAISE. Calm down.

SUSANNE. No! Ted never could see why some art had to be destroyed. *(Lighting a match)*

BLAISE. They're not your best work. True.

SUSANNE. I spent seven months making paintings I despised. I created monsters, and I want them killed!

(She thrusts sketches into the fireplace.)

BLAISE. God. Don't do that.

SUSANNE. I didn't want to hang this. Ted tore it out my hands.

BLAISE. Stop shouting.

SUSANNE. The painting is a shroud, and nothing happens till—

BLAISE. Enough!

SUSANNE. The spirit returns, and the painter gets back inside. I hate them! Hate! Hate! *(Sobs)* Can't you...

BLAISE. Okay, Susanne.

WHITE SUITS IN SUMMER

SUSANNE. Burn the paintings for me?

(BLAISE downs liquor. Takes a match to the fireplace.)

BLAISE. There. I'm burning—

SUSANNE. We're burning them!

BLAISE. Right. We're doing it.

SUSANNE. Oh yes. Yes. Now people can remember me like I was.

(Ambulance sirens come louder and louder. **SUSANNE** *runs out.* **TED** *rushes on stage, followed by* **LUCILLE.***)*

TED. That's the ambulance.

BLAISE. *(Crossing down and looking out)* It's here.

LUCILLE. Oh God, it's time.

NURSE. *(offstage)* Make way, everyone.

MALE VOICE #1. *(offstage)* We're coming through. COMING THROUGH.

WHITE SUITS IN SUMMER

Scene Two

(Later that day. The gallery glows in afternoon light. **BLAISE** *is reviewing a book.* **LUCILLE** *enters lugging a man's suitcase, bags, and canes.* **BLAISE** *goes to embrace her, but she backs off.)*

BLAISE. Your uncle died?

LUCILLE. Lord. Oh. Yes. During the Last Rites, Uncle couldn't breathe; I needed you.

BLAISE. Didn't you get my message?

LUCILLE. Don't. The Bible says honor your relatives—

BLAISE. It also says don't lie. *(Smiles vaguely)*

LUCILLE. Kindness is something your family either taught you or not. You needn't feel nice, but you should act nice—

BLAISE. Janus-faced.

LUCILLE. The service is Wednesday morning, for those interested. Uncle's last words were: "Where's Blaise?" He wanted me to have a real partner. *(Fumbles out a plastic bag)* The attorney gave me these trinkets: some spoons, Uncle's rings and his watch, and his will. *(Hands* **BLAISE** *the will)*

BLAISE. You want me to read it?

LUCILLE. Sure.

*(***BLAISE*** reads. His face pales.)*

LUCILLE. What's wrong?

BLAISE. I don't know how to—God—

LUCILLE. *(Grabbing the will)* The entire estate goes to the Dominicans except for... What's this? He's willing me—these pearl-handled spoons?

BLAISE. The bastard went through with it. Here I felt...

WHITE SUITS IN SUMMER

LUCILLE. I can't...believe it—

BLAISE. If I stayed away—He might leave you something—

LUCILLE. Oh, my Lord. Mercy. Oh, no.

BLAISE. You look weak.

LUCILLE. There hasn't been time to tell you with all the commotion...but I took a pregnancy test.

BLAISE. It's just...We've barely had sex.

LUCILLE. The doctor said it's unlikely. We'll have the results later today. Don't be depressed, I can't take it if you are. A woman always fears she'll miss out— Since we've been home you...neglect me to share confidences with Susanne.

BLAISE. God! Don't talk this way.

LUCILLE. Are you screwing her?

BLAISE. No. You're overwrought.

LUCILLE. I'm falling apart. Uncle tried to set things straight. He tried and tried to talk to you...

BLAISE. Don't punish me because your mean uncle—

LUCILLE. You dawdle with nowhere plans— Why do this to us?

BLAISE. I'm going out. *(Grabs a cigarette)*

LUCILLE. I needed you at the hospital and I need you now. Marriage means being there. *(LUCILLE looks around with dismay;* **BLAISE** *puts on his tennis shoes)* You can't just waste hours with some part you may never play. *(Picks up the empty portfolio)* Where are Susanne's paintings?

BLAISE. *Disparus*, as the French would say... I—We burned them.

LUCILLE. *(Horrified)* Not possible.

WHITE SUITS IN SUMMER

BLAISE. Susanne couldn't bear seeing...art she hated.

LUCILLE. *(Stunned)* They were priceless.

SOUND: The phone rings. Blaise answers it.

BLAISE. It's Blaise...Yeah...

LUCILLE. Artists must separate ego from art. Art claims its own life. You can't destroy it because the artist isn't—in the same place— *(Irritated)* Tell whoever's calling about Uncle.

BLAISE. *(Into the phone)* I love the part. They're paying that much? When? *(Hangs up; to* **LUCILLE***)* Some friends are starting a summer theater. They've been calling me.

LUCILLE. Where? Why didn't you say something?

BLAISE. New York. I want US to go.

LUCILLE. Now?

BLAISE. I don't want to turn into all I've hated. I'd rather do everything bad and get caught.

LUCILLE. We have to clean out Uncle's place.

BLAISE. The Dominicans can do it. There's nothing holding us, sweetie. You can visit anytime, but I'm never coming back—ever...You said you'd support—

LUCILLE. Opportunity, at the right time—

BLAISE. Every day I do what I have to and you look sadder.

LUCILLE. Your talent won't take care of us.

BLAISE. I'm beginning to hate the sight of this house—with the big mortgage. Here, I'll assign you my interest.

LUCILLE. I won't live in some rattrap.

WHITE SUITS IN SUMMER

BLAISE. I never asked that—

LUCILLE. I can, could, and probably will leave Exposition Boulevard soon.

BLAISE. Good girl.

LUCILLE. But we don't have to leave it now.

BLAISE. I won't let property trap us. I'm an artist.

LUCILLE. Says who? Sorry.

BLAISE. I'm going. *(Haltingly)* You'll come?

LUCILLE. I need to hire a good lawyer. Uncle was out of his mind when he made this will. Undue influence is how it happened.

BLAISE. I'm heading back. Eventually something is going to hit. If I keep pushing, I'll keep finding. I've got the drive—

LUCILLE. You're crazy.

BLAISE. I'm not sure but I'll act in my best interest—

LUCILLE. Self-absorbed—

BLAISE. And from that strength.

LUCILLE. Reckless—

BLAISE. I won't be fooled!

(Exits)

(A bit later, the house phone rings and **LUCILLE** *gets it.* **TED** *enters carrying a large box.* **LUCILLE** *gasps at his miserably timed appearance. She hangs up the phone.)*

LUCILLE. Susanne's not here.

WHITE SUITS IN SUMMER

TED. What's wrong?

LUCILLE. Uncle died. Blaise's moving. I'm disinherited.

TED. All in one day?

LUCILLE. And I found out I'm not pregnant.

TED. Maybe that's a good thing.

LUCILLE. I'm by myself now.

TED. I need your help. *(Lifts one of* **SUSANNE***'s drawings from the box)* Do you recognize this?

LUCILLE. My eyes are blurry.

TED. Discarded sketches. I've retrieved hundreds. Could you organize them? Take over her lectures?

LUCILLE. I'm starting to cry...

TED. You know her work better than anyone.

LUCILLE. First, I need to confront this letter. *(Hands it to* **TED***)* Read it? After his will, I can't bear to.

TED. It's from your uncle.

LUCILLE. I'm his only heir and he gives all to the Church.

TED. *(Reads)* "Dear Lucille, You and Blaise need to start out on your own."

LUCILLE. Nasty!

TED. *(Reads)* "Still, your aunt and I wanted you alone to have this bag."

LUCILLE. Worthless heirlooms—

TED. *(Reads)* "Special spoons for a special heart." Uncle Gene.

WHITE SUITS IN SUMMER

LUCILLE. Rusted silver...

TED. A few dollars a spoon.

LUCILLE. *(Opens bag)* What's this? Oh!

TED. A paper?

LUCILLE. Heavenly mother! Oh, no?

TED. *(Takes the paper)* It's a life insurance policy for—

LUCILLE. Six, seven...

TED. Eight figures.

LUCILLE. Oh, no!

TED. You're the beneficiary.

LUCILLE. Good Lord! There must be some mistake.

TED. There's your name. The policy is paid in full.

LUCILLE. It's a miracle! Oh, my!

TED. Fabulous!

LUCILLE. I'll pay off the mortgage. I can live here like—

TED. You did before! Great.

LUCILLE. We'll start a tradition.

TED. A new artist a month at Exposition Boulevard.

LUCILLE. Oh, my God. Mercy. Yes.

TED. But can the heiress still do Susanne's lectures?

LUCILLE. You haven't canceled anything yet?

WHITE SUITS IN SUMMER

TED. No.

LUCILLE. We'll create a retrospective with Tulane.

TED. Mother will be delighted.

LUCILLE. We'll work upstairs, clear out Uncle's quarters.

TED. Wonderful!

(They continue to plan as they exit.)

*(**SOUND**: From the Cathedral we hear a hymn like, "City of God." "Let us build the City of God, May our tears be turned into dancing, For the Lord, our Light and our Love, has turned the night into day.")*

*(Moments later **BLAISE** walks in to pack. **SUSANNE** enters nervously, looks at the park.)*

SUSANNE. Beautiful night... Starry skies. Moon's coming up over the park. It rained earlier and we needed the rain... Oh...is that Ted with Lucille?

BLAISE. *(Looking out)* Who knows?...I'm leaving.

SUSANNE. You work on a short fuse.

BLAISE. The essence of flight is immediacy.

SUSANNE. You're leaving to do a play?

BLAISE. Something like that.

SUSANNE. I once ran off with a guy who promised me a string of pearls. I did what I was supposed to do, but—

BLAISE. People don't pay you well in the theater I work in.

SUSANNE. You owe me pearls.

BLAISE. It pays in the high two figures like an allowance. The smart actor—

WHITE SUITS IN SUMMER

SUSANNE. I'm dreaming of you—

BLAISE. Makes you buy a ticket to see him.

SUSANNE. Your touch—

BLAISE. I can't think of one successful actor with a—

SUSANNE. Your body—

BLAISE. Happy home life. One of my friends is in drug rehab—

SUSANNE. To me you are—the sound of leaves stirring—

BLAISE. Another jumped off the Mississippi River Bridge—

SUSANNE. Water over cool stones—

BLAISE. My most stable friend had a nervous breakdown—

SUSANNE. You arouse the dark side of my soul. Say I can come, Blaise. Just say—I can come.

(He takes her in his arms, kisses her, repeating, "okay.")

*(**SOUND**: A melancholy refrain from something like, "The City of God" is heard from the Cathedral. "Let us build the City of God, May our tears be turned into dancing, For the Lord, our Light and our Love, has turned the night into day.")*

(curtain)

WHITE SUITS IN SUMMER

APPENDIX

Replace the opening scene with this text.

Characters

BLAISE SALATICH: A handsome, out-of-work actor, 28
LUCILLE: His serious wife, an art critic, 38
SUSANNE DUPRÉ: His ex-lover a famous painter, 28
TED CLAPPER: Her frustrated manager, 26
NURSE
3 METER MAIDS
FEMALE COP
COOK
6 DOMINICAN SINGING NUNS

Setting

A mansion on Exposition Boulevard, New Orleans. We are in a big, finely-proportioned parlor with a high ceiling, Orientals, a crystal chandelier. The atmosphere is that of a grand sanctuary, where the landowner can view Audubon Park as a superior. Floor-to-ceiling windows, sometimes used as entrances, open onto a gallery overlooking a wide lawn, which tumbles onto Audubon Park. During the daytime one has the feeling of a semi-tropical park, and at night of an oak garden, which climbs into the stars.

Time

The present. Sunshine, already hard on the windows, fills the room with a sharp light.

WHITE SUITS IN SUMMER

ACT ONE

Scene One

(A summer day. Noon. The present. Several suitcases line the stage.)

(At rise: **LUCILLE**, *28, runs onstage. She's very healthy with a mass of hair and deep-set hazel eyes. There is a curious blend of country carelessness and intelligence. Her husband,* **BLAISE**, *enters, buttoning his shirt. He is handsome, about 26, but his carriage makes him appear older. He is tall, long-limbed with a wide forehead, thick brown hair, and fine sensitive eyes. He wears conservative dark clothes, obviously expensive, and he wears them well. Harsh sunlight falls over the gallery as* **TED CLAPPER**, *in a rumpled white suit, approaches. He checks back for fear his car will be towed. An effusive businessman, he's in his twenties, but his face looks older.)*

TED. Anybody home? *(Crosses to* **BLAISE***)* Teddy Clapper.

LUCILLE. Who?

TED. New Orleans Country Club? Southern Yacht Club? Now I'm managing Susanne Dupré.

LUCILLE. Susanne Dupré. *(Screams in delight)* Oh my. Oh God. Oh, no.

TED. *(Searches about)* My glasses broke. I've a second pair.

LUCILLE. I'll fix them. You know my husband. *(To herself)* Oh my God. Susanne Dupré.

BLAISE. Can I help you with something?

TED. Mom and I want you to host an exposition of Susanne Dupré.

LUCILLE. *(to* **BLAISE***)* This is the miracle we've been waiting for.

(Three **METER MAIDS** *walk across the stage talking loudly over their ipods)*

TED. *(Looks out)* They're not giving me a ticket? I double-parked by a fire hydrant, then barged into the curb...

WHITE SUITS IN SUMMER

BLAISE. You should move your car.

TED. Like I said, we're looking for patrons to do an exposition of...

(Phone rings. **TED** *searches for phone, gives up when ringing stops.)*

TED. Mom might phone. I've rough car trips calling her. She fired the night watchman and bought me a phone. My mother is the sweetest, panicked person on earth. I advanced up to escort when Dad departed this world...

LUCILLE. I saw it in the obituaries.

TED. A show on Exposition Boulevard could be an important event. Susanne's a young legend.

LUCILLE. A practitioner of the—

TED. Nobler forms.

LUCILLE. Her show in Berlin left me—

TED. Ecstatic as did her show at the—

LUCILLE and **TED.** *(Together)* Guggenheim in New York.

*(***TED***'s cell phone rings. He waves it off.)*

TED. We'll ignore that. All Mom's friends are dying, so it's not great for her. Her two best friends died within weeks. What with her heart surgery and the cataracts...

(Phone stops ringing. He searches for the scrapbook and pictures.)

TED. Mom made a scrapbook of your wedding. She keeps saying, "Why couldn't you've married Lucille." *(to* **LUCILLE***)* Every boy at Jesuit High School was in love with you.

BLAISE. *(to* **TED***)* Thanks for the gift.

LUCILLE. *(to* **TED***)* Your glasses fixed.

WHITE SUITS IN SUMMER

TED. Amazing. *(Phone rings,* **TED** *answers it)* Hello there. *(To* **BLAISE***)* If I don't respond instantly, Mom calls the cops. *(Talks into the phone)* Yeah, Mom. I gave Lucille the clippings and the...no. *(To himself)* Where are those grapefruit spoons? *(Checks about; to* **LUCILLE***)* Mom had them replaced. *(To* **BLAISE***)* My family's in fine jewelry and heirlooms. *(Into phone)* I got them. *(Hangs up)*

LUCILLE. *(Peeking in the box)* Another priceless treasure from Uncle.

TED. Mom says ya'll have the finest art collection.

BLAISE. He gave it to the museum.

(Phone rings, but **TED** *ignores it, looking for an outlet to recharge it.)*

TED. If I'm gone long, she'll find me—hunt me down. My sister came for a month with her kids—wild, exhausting six, seven, and twelve-year-olds. After she left, it required weeks of down time to revive Mother.

LUCILLE. Wouldn't it be wonderful to have kids 'round the house?

TED. Little Lucilles and—

BLAISE. We're not having children yet.

LUCILLE. I didn't mean today.

TED. Where's that outlet?

BLAISE. With Uncle Gene's illness and—

LUCILLE. Blaise's goal is to become a great actor, get fame, start his own production company.

TED. *(Interrupting, to* **BLAISE***)* Say, weren't you and Susanne schoolmates at—?

BLAISE. Berkeley.

TED. Right. I told Susanne a political edge would move her ahead faster. She started her triangle series in Berlin.

WHITE SUITS IN SUMMER

(Blaise guides him to an outlet.)

LUCILLE. Splendid.

TED. I organized this smashing opening at the Mary Boon in New York. She constructed and deconstructed Naughty Marietta and the Casket Girls at the Whitney. *(TED's phone rings)* Mom gets foggy and keeps calling. *(Speaks into the phone)* I'll pick you up for dinner.

(He hangs up. Phone rings again. **TED** *throws up his hands.)*

TED. Each time, it's an earnest pitch—when can I expect you? Mom's got a housekeeper, a chauffeur, and a cook, but she's essentially alone. Eating out and her poodle, "Bootsy," are all that keep her going. Pardon me. *(Picks up the phone and talks to his Mom)* Yes, I gave them the—no, no. I'll do it. More gifts—certificates for silver frames for your wedding portrait and invitation, and for baby rattles, cups, brushes, diaper pins, cutlery, and dishes. All to be engraved later.

LUCILLE. How extravagant.

TED. We've tons of wedding and baby gifts—never bought or returned—and Mom wants you to have them all—in case something... She should never have had heart surgery of that magnitude. *(Into the phone)* Yes. She's got it. Goodbye, Mom. *(Hangs up the phone)* I handle Mom's expenses, the understatement of the year. Time's coming when I'll have to move in—

BLAISE. *(Checks his watch)* Excuse me.

TED. Wait. About the show—

LUCILLE. 'Course we'll sponsor it. We'll use the side gallery.

TED. Excellent.

LUCILLE. Uncle will contribute. I've got great ambitions for Blaise.

(3 **METER MAIDS** *enter the street yelling and writing up tickets)*

TED. Is that a meter maid out there?

METER MAIDS. You get that clunker. Up on the curb ? Fire Hydrant.

WHITE SUITS IN SUMMER

(A female **COP** *joins them)*

COP. No Parking and Handicapped Zone!

TED. *(Hearing their voices)* What? They-ve got a—Stop!

LUCILLE. Don't leave.

TED. Three shapes of them are ticketing my car. Bat women from hell. *(To* **LUCILLE***)* I'll be right back.

BLAISE. Take your time. I'm going for a smoke. *(Exits)*

(Moments later. **LUCILLE***, high-strung, turns up a baby-minder, a ritual she deals with continually.)*

*(**SOUND**: Uncle Gene, moaning in his room.* **LUCILLE** *speaks into the machine.)*

LUCILLE. Nurse?

*(**LUCILLE** gets up and paces, looks out the window, to where* **TED** *has gone then back upstage.)*

NURSE. *(Entering)* Yes. Miss Lucille

LUCILLE. Can't you ease Uncle's pain?

NURSE. Got a call in to the doctor. I've been having a time—. The man won't—you try getting him to—

LUCILLE. *(Dismissing her)* Tell Cook to serve some condiments.

NURSE. She don't like to leave that kitchen!

LUCILLE. Tell her!

*(**NURSE** exits)*

WHITE SUITS IN SUMMER

(SUSANNE, 24, enters, quietly with her portfolio and paint box. She is dressed casually in seductive clothes. Hollows shadow her cheeks and her slender neck. There is a quality of nervous tension, the mental strain of an artist who puts unrelieved pressure on herself.)

SUSANNE. Hi. I'm Susanne Dupré.

LUCILLE. Oh my. Oh my Lord. You're an absolutely brilliant artist. I'm Lucille, Blaise's wife.

SUSANNE. Hello. Ted sent me in.

LUCILLE. Anyone in love with painting admires your work. *(Looks about)* Where's Ted?

SUSANNE. Parking the car. Is this a bad time?

LUCILLE. Sorry—I'm in such a tether.

SUSANNE. I understand. My challenge is to discern reality.

LUCILLE. Ah. To paint things the way they truly are—

SUSANNE. Not through false glasses.

LUCILLE. New Orleans must be quite an interesting study when—

SUSANNE. Viewed as an outsider. *(Stares at her)* You're lovely. *(Overcome with disappointment)* I don't think I can exhibit here. It's too—fussy.

(SUSANNE looks out, her face hot and sweating.)

(SOUND: Music floats in from the Cathedral, something like Isaiah 6: "Here I am, Lord. Is it I, Lord? I have heard you calling in the night. I will go, Lord, if you lead me. I will hold your people in my heart.")

LUCILLE. Choir practice from Holy Name Church. I can hear them even better from my classroom at Tulane.

SUSANNE. *(Avoiding* **LUCILLE***'s face)* You teach?

WHITE SUITS IN SUMMER

LUCILLE. Art history. At Tulane.

SUSANNE. What a view. The sun sifting through Spanish moss. And the park dancing all around. I feel like I'm being reborn, nourished by Utopia. People would be calmer if they lived in beauty. Marvelous house.

LUCILLE. It's been in my family for generations.

SUSANNE. And will stay there.

LUCILLE. These houses are great 'cause they keep memory alive. *(Moaning through baby-minder)* My uncle has cancer.

SUSANNE. Sorry.

LUCILLE. I use a baby-minder. It's sad.

SUSANNE. With a certain—

LUCILLE. If you need to buffer entropy, this is a good training ground.

SUSANNE. My presence feels inappropriate.

LUCILLE. I adored your Berlin exhibit. "How the Feminist and the Archetype Intersect."

SUSANNE. What did your husband think?

LUCILLE. Right. You met Blaise.

SUSANNE. Well?

LUCILLE. He framed my article comparing your painting to Beckett's drama. *(Hands* **SUSANNE** *the article)*

SUSANNE. "Apocalyptic Isolation." Some title.

LUCILLE. You're a prodigy.

SUSANNE. People get noticed if they do something unusual and live in New York in their twenties.

WHITE SUITS IN SUMMER

LUCILLE. You're welcome to stay—

SUSANNE. There is motion here, but again—it's not the house I was hoping for.

LUCILLE. We could paint the walls, redo some lights.

SUSANNE. *(Shaking her head)* No.

LUCILLE. Blaise needs to meet people in the arts.

SUSANNE. It won't work.

LUCILLE. He wants to do leads in film and theater, the whole panoramic portrait.

SUSANNE. Not tiny parts, shards in the mosaic.

LUCILLE. We can create projects for you both from here.

SUSANNE. *(Picks up a large white album)* Your wedding album.

LUCILLE. There's Blaise kissing me at the altar, feeding me cake.

SUSANNE. You're still newlyweds. Love hasn't changed to respect.

(SUSANNE fidgets with a cigarette. TED enters.)

TED. I can't stay. I promised to take Mom to Antoine's.

LUCILLE. Don't worry. Susanne and I can discuss the exposition.

SUSANNE. If we have one.

TED. Don't mind her. *(Whispers to SUSANNE)* You'll do what I say.

SUSANNE. I don't know. *(To herself)* Change carries consequence.

TED. I'm off.

WHITE SUITS IN SUMMER

(LUCILLE ushers **TED** *to the door.* **BLAISE** *enters from the park, brushes past* **SUSANNE**, *walks to get liquor.)*

BLAISE. Oh, Susanne.

LUCILLE. Right. You knew each other. Kiss me, dear. *(He kisses her)* We're still honeymooning.

BLAISE. Excuse me. *(Leaving)*

LUCILLE. Don't be rude, darling. I need your input on the exposition.

SUSANNE. Maybe you shouldn't have it, just enjoy the park, and—

BLAISE. Can I get you a drink? Every Southern home has a recovery shelf. *(To* **SUSANNE***)* A Bloody Mary?

SUSANNE. Perrier. Might as well drink with class.

LUCILLE. You'll let us host you?

SUSANNE. Not sure. I feel mostly good about what Ted and I are doing— It's simply a desire for a real home—that the other galleries can't fulfill.

BLAISE. Maybe this need is invalid.

SUSANNE. I think not—

*(***BLAISE** *wipes his forehead, which has broken out in a sweat.* **COOK** *enters with a tray of condiments. Plops them on a table.)*

COOK. This ain't part of my job!

*(***COOK** *exits.* **LUCILLE** *chuckles in the embarrassed silence and passes condiments.)*

LUCILLE. *(To* **SUSANNE***)* Your use of triangles intrigues me. We must include "Shakti's Heart"—your triangle symbolizing the Hindu Goddess.

BLAISE. It's too Gauguin for me. Actually, that piece depresses me the least.

WHITE SUITS IN SUMMER

LUCILLE. Blaise!

BLAISE. *(To* **SUSANNE***)* Weren't you supposed to search out dark, lugubrious triangles?

SUSANNE. The easy expositions are over, and the tough ones just begun.

LUCILLE. Showing here will not be as difficult as you think.

*(***BLAISE** *starts to exit.)*

LUCILLE. You're not leaving? Relax, dear. This is for you.

BLAISE. I like to pace. If I sit, I might miss something.

LUCILLE. *(Clears her throat)* Tell us about your recent work.

SUSANNE. I've been correcting energy-draining behaviors.

LUCILLE. That affects your painting.

SUSANNE. And life. Confusion won't divert me from seeing reality.

LUCILLE. Your paintings are sharper.

SUSANNE. Painting is about paying attention in a Buddhist way.

BLAISE. That's hard to do.

SUSANNE. I slip into the skin of people I see—even if it hurts.

LUCILLE. You paint "fruitful blank spaces" which life fills in.

SUSANNE. When I smile...I'm thinking of something enticing.

LUCILLE. You're smiling now? Isn't she, honey?

SUSANNE. You can use art to heal, to face a part of yourself you hate.

LUCILLE. Go on!

WHITE SUITS IN SUMMER

SUSANNE. In my last triangle series, I saw myself in the colors and mended my ways.

LUCILLE. *(To* **SUSANNE***)* How do you know when a painting is finished?

SUSANNE. *(To* **BLAISE***)* When you love it.

(A moan through the baby-minder. A bell rings. **LUCILLE** *rises to leave.)*

LUCILLE. Uncle calls every five minutes.

BLAISE. Nurse is there.

LUCILLE. Yes, but he waits for me. *(To* **BLAISE***)* Darling, get Susanne's press agent, mailing lists. Talk strategy.

SUSANNE. I don't know.

LUCILLE. We'll give you two an outrageous reception: jazz band, oysters etoufees, mint juleps.

SUSANNE. But does the world need another show?

LUCILLE. 'Course. Artists make dreams. *(To* **BLAISE***)* Kiss, kiss, love bug.

*(***LUCILLE** *adjusts the baby-minder and flutters off.* **BLAISE** *gives* **SUSANNE** *a hard look.)*

SUSANNE. Love bug.

BLAISE. When did you move to New Orleans?

SUSANNE. Before your wedding.

BLAISE. You came to our wedding?

SUSANNE. *(Removes newspaper notice)* I sat in back of the church. Didn't make the reception.

(Doorbell rings.)

WHITE SUITS IN SUMMER

NURSE. *(Offstage)* The prescription. I've got it, Miss Lucille.

(BLAISE turns down the baby-minder.)

SUSANNE. Lucille is, like a mother... You think about California?

BLAISE. I recall lots of dead things. *(Starts to leave)*

SUSANNE. After your wedding, I slept all day. I felt like a part of me was melting—

BLAISE. Now you've seen me and I've seen you.

SUSANNE. Why did you move here? For the?

BLAISE. Restaurants—You can be a starving artist in your teens, but in your twenties you like to dine out occasionally.

SUSANNE. When I started painting, I didn't worry about sales.

BLAISE. As long as you work for your soul, it's great.

SUSANNE. Sometimes I can't—sleep.

BLAISE. You need to—

SUSANNE. I'm not taking pills or fooling around.

(LUCILLE enters with mail to get a bottle of gin.)

LUCILLE. The mail came.

BLAISE. My headshots!

LUCILLE. Why send them? Soon, we'll produce you here. Money's the crucial factor.

SUSANNE. And talent.

LUCILLE. Persistence. I won't let Blaise fail. *(Pause)* Uncle wants a Ramos Gin Fizz made of orange flower, water, and gin.

WHITE SUITS IN SUMMER

BLAISE. I'll get it.

LUCILLE. *(Checks the baby-minder)* You plan which paintings to hang. *(Moaning through the baby-minder; she starts to go)* Everything's an argument with Uncle. Is there any nutritional value in gin?

SUSANNE. *(To* **BLAISE***)* Joy and celebration.

LUCILLE. Mm. I can hardly get one job done when something hits me. *(Kisses him boldly)*

BLAISE. I should help you.

LUCILLE. Give me a kiss, pumpkin. A bear kiss. *(Pause—exits)*

(A breeze rises. **BLAISE** *gazes at* **SUSANNE** *so the light from the great porch lanterns catches her face with streaks of brightness. Distant thunder. The gallery is blanketed with a golden coppery light.)*

*(**SONG**: A hymn floats from the Cathedral, something like On Eagle's Wings. "And he will raise you up on eagle's wings. And hold you in the palm of his hand.")*

SUSANNE. *(Sings)* "And he will raise you up. And he will raise you up. And he will raise you up...on the last day." I love rain on an unexpected day. Every pore opens to the wind.

BLAISE. Nice.

SUSANNE. That's what I remember about New Orleans. The music—and the rain.

BLAISE. I don't have time for this.

*(**SOUND**: Thunder.)*

SUSANNE. There's a sense of romance about the rain. The sun is around us, but the rain is within us. *(Removes her sketchbook, draws)* When I got here, the rain seized me. Mind if I draw you?

WHITE SUITS IN SUMMER

(She moves closer, drawing him. Footsteps inside. **BLAISE** *calls out.)*

BLAISE. Who's there?

SUSANNE. I'm putting you in a triangle—

BLAISE. Lucille? *(Picks up a book)*

SUSANNE. Using weightlessness to let your image soar.

BLAISE. Five minutes is all.

SUSANNE. You've a wonderful body.

(With a flickering smile, **BLAISE** *clutches his book like a Bible.)*

BLAISE. I read one self-help book a week—

SUSANNE. Dressed or undressed—

BLAISE. <u>The Greatest Salesman Alive</u>, takes a year to finish 'cause it's—

SUSANNE. Self-hypnosis.

BLAISE. You read one chapter three times a day for a month.

SUSANNE. What contacts do you have here?

BLAISE. None. I'm competitive with people.

SUSANNE. Hold that pose.

BLAISE. I forget how I'm supposed to behave.

*(***BLAISE** *gives Susanne a hard, silencing look.)*

SUSANNE. When I saw you in "Hamlet", you defined the word, star.

(She takes out his picture as Hamlet. **LUCILLE** *hurries onstage.)*

LUCILLE. We've lovely watercress sandwiches and crab soup. Give me a kiss.

WHITE SUITS IN SUMMER

(**LUCILLE** *kisses him)* Oh Lord. She's painting here.

BLAISE. Stay and watch.

LUCILLE. Ooh. Uncle won't eat 'less I join him.

BLAISE. *(to* **LUCILLE***)* I'm tired. Let's go nap.

SUSANNE. I should let you two alone.

LUCILLE. Don't be silly. Uncle cries out for attention. His paper is damp. His milk is warm. There's dust on the floor. The new maid is lazy. She barely came in the month we were gone. Then I've got to prepare the shopping list.

BLAISE. Let me help you.

LUCILLE. No. Sit for Susanne. You know how Uncle treats the nurse when I'm not there.

(**LUCILLE** *buzzes off.* **BLAISE** *follows uneasily, stands in the doorway as the night turns black.* **SUSANNE** *toys with a palette knife. Seeing it,* **BLAISE** *trembles.* **SUSANNE** *speaks maliciously.)*

SUSANNE. You've broken out in a sweat.

BLAISE. New Orleans is melting me.

SUSANNE. How long have you been unemployed? Eight months?

BLAISE. Warm.

SUSANNE. Nine?

BLAISE. Warmer.

SUSANNE. A year? Two?

BLAISE. "Regret not the glitter of any lost day." Tennessee Williams.

SUSANNE. What happened in Hollywood?

WHITE SUITS IN SUMMER

BLAISE. Nothing.

SUSANNE. You told Lucille you'd talk—

BLAISE. I thought I'd make a bundle.

SUSANNE. Doing what?

BLAISE. Selling chunks of my soul at varying intervals.

SUSANNE. Did you?

BLAISE. I auditioned weekly for months.

SUSANNE. That's a lot of no's.

BLAISE. I was holding on for the word, yes—

SUSANNE. *(Slyly)* To lose yourself in the play?

BLAISE. Right.

SUSANNE. You went to interviews with producers?

BLAISE. Yes.

SUSANNE. Casting directors?

BLAISE. So.

SUSANNE. Ah, Blaise Salatich. You've played all these parts blah-blah-blah.

BLAISE. Exactly.

SUSANNE. Finally, a director of a major picture hires you and he gets fired!

BLAISE. Who told you that?

SUSANNE. Did you go back to the old ways?

BLAISE. No.

WHITE SUITS IN SUMMER

SUSANNE. Numbing yourself with—?

BLAISE. No. I wanted to, by God.

SUSANNE. But you didn't.

BLAISE. I kept busy, worked out. Ran.

(He feels for a cigarette. She takes it out for him.)

SUSANNE. You didn't slip once after so many months?

BLAISE. Never.

SUSANNE. So you auditioned for special parts.

BLAISE. Right.

SUSANNE. You were a hand model? A parts model? What?

BLAISE. Soft porn is what they call it. So.

SUSANNE. What happened on your last audition?

BLAISE. Producer arrives in this enormous barrel-like hat.

SUSANNE. He asked you to his hotel room.

BLAISE. Devouring pistachio nuts, telling me his tale of woe.

(SUSANNE hands him a drink.)

BLAISE. Asks me to sit on the bed and unbutton my shirt...This can't be happening, I thought. I was anxious, but it was a lead. "I'd like to cast you," he said. So, I took off my shirt. He stared till my ears got hot. This can't be happening, I thought. He made me lie on the bed. Then he undid my belt and unzipped my pants. This can't be happening. I backed off. There was this screaming, this hotness. He came at me with a knife. Blood everywhere, drenching his shirt, pants, the floor. Looked like he was coming at himself with the knife.

WHITE SUITS IN SUMMER

SUSANNE. He died.

BLAISE. I'm trashed in California.

(SUSANNE adds ice to his drink. A song like Here I am, Lord is heard from the church.)

LUCILLE. *(Entering)* Uncle wants ice chips for his drink. Your sketch is rapturous. *(Looking at* **SUSANNE***'s drawing)*

BLAISE. *(To* **LUCILLE***)* Stay, sweetheart.

LUCILLE. Did Susanne agree to—

SUSANNE. I do!

LUCILLE. Glorious.

(LUCILLE exits.)

SUSANNE. You have an agent here?

BLAISE. She calls herself one. The only help I ever got was from other artists. They taught me how to face guerilla warfare, to be outspoken, aggressive.

SUSANNE. You can't be an artist unless you plunge ahead. Courage brings peace. Dream big. Fight back. Nirvana awaits. When you march forward, you stand up for the weak, the old, the silenced poets of the world.
(A car horn toots. **SUSANNE** *starts, and crosses to* **BLAISE***.)*

SUSANNE. I have to go. Ted gets impatient.

BLAISE. I've missed you.

*(***BLAISE** *smiles sadly. The car toots again.* **SUSANNE** *hurries out.* **LUCILLE** *enters with an envelope.)*

LUCILLE. Good news. Uncle's financing the exposition.

BLAISE. *(Sarcastically)* Victory is ours.

WHITE SUITS IN SUMMER

LUCILLE. Ours? Did you drink all this gin?

BLAISE. It's a negotiable indulgence. *(Hands her an envelope)*

LUCILLE. Oh dear.

BLAISE. Why does Uncle send you business letters? You talk all day.

LUCILLE. He's a Soniat. Soon as they have an opinion, it becomes a legal document.

BLAISE. Throw it away.

LUCILLE. Wait, it's a lien on this house. He didn't mention—

BLAISE. He was annoyed, you said—

LUCILLE. With your career and our stay abroad.

BLAISE. But he gave us the house.

LUCILLE. Before he did—he took out a mortgage—

BLAISE. "You don't have to be rich," he said, "when your relatives are rich."

LUCILLE. To pay some of his insurance.

(Doorbell rings.)

(Six **DOMINICAN NUNS** *arrive in full habits.* **NURSE** *lets them in.)*

NUNS. Good evening. Is our patient's sleeping?

NURSE. Finally. I've never seen so many habits!

NUNS. The good priests sponsored this call—

LUCILLE. *(To* **BLAISE***)* Dominicans slinking about...badmouthing you to Uncle.

WHITE SUITS IN SUMMER

COOK. *(Poking in)* I ain't cooking for more people!

(LUCILLE goes to the NUNS.)

LUCILLE. You'll have to come back—

NUNS. We're here to sing for your Uncle and leave our music!

(The NUNS hand NURSE an envelope and burst into a jazzy rendition of "Amazing Grace." BLAISE tries to usher them out)

BLAISE. Good night—

LUCILLE. Thank you.

NUNS. And we brought pictures of the our new music hall that your Uncle wants to sponsor—

COOK. *(Poking in)* I'll bring him supper and—

NUNS. Put our folder by his food tray. With our blessing.

(BLAISE seizes the envelope, opens it, and reads)

BLAISE. *(Reads)* "Addendum to the will and testament of Gene Soniat. I hereby leave the Dominican order—"

LUCILLE. Y'all are writing Uncle's will?

NUNS. We put in a sentence for what he wants to give to the convent. And a rosary blessed by the Vatican and a large print Bible—*(to LUCILLE)* Of course you are the major heir although he is upset about your husband. *(Pointedly)* He keeps asking for you, Blaise.—It would be wise to visit with him.

BLAISE. *(Starting to leave)* I'm not going to be two-faced—

NUNS. *(To LUCILLE)* We brought Gregorian chants for when he—

BLAISE. Get out! Just get the—

NUNS. He says you married Lucille for his money, that acting is for—

WHITE SUITS IN SUMMER

BLAISE. For parasites?

NUNS. —If you can't get your own sponsors, you should quit.

BLAISE. Everyone wants to be a performer or—. Then we have religious institutions grabbing the money. Crappy singers working for free and alienating a dwindling public.

LUCILLE. Don't lose patience...

NUNS. The lord is bountiful. Help your uncle to understand you. Visit him. Say you're interested in sales.

BLAISE. I'm not getting in that pot. The last man who got in there got eaten.

(Laughs, but **LUCILLE** *doesn't join in.)*

NUNS. *(Looking at* **LUCILLE***)* We promised your wife we'd get you to chat with him.

BLAISE. Honey... have you been talking to these...these—sisters!

LUCILLE. You know Uncle's...sick. That's why he's irritable, and can't be with anyone more than five minutes. I love him. I remember how he was when I was a little girl. I can't think of life without— He's not himself—

NUNS. Now he's dying.

BLAISE. Are we sure? God!

NUNS. We moved him to our final rites list.

LUCILLE. Lord, I can't take it.

NUNS. Has he signed a living will? *(To* **BLAISE***)* Poke your head in the door. Go talk to him! Or Lucille may be disowned.

(We hear Uncle moan through the baby monitor)

NUNS. Let's go to him!

WHITE SUITS IN SUMMER

(LUCILLE exits with the NUNS who intone "Amazing Grace" as they bow their heads and head toward Uncle's room)

(BLAISE gazes after them, breathes deeply. We hear wind from a summer rainstorm, sweeping over the park. He picks up the book, and exits. Lights fade.)

Also by
Rosary Hartel O'Neill...

The Awakening of Kate Chopin

Black Jack: The Thief of Possession

Degas in New Orleans

John Singer Sargent and Madame X

Marilyn/God

Property

Solitaire

Turtle Soup

Uncle Victor

White Suits in Summer

The Wings of Madness

Wishing Aces

Please visit our website **samuelfrench.com** for complete descriptions and licensing information.

www.ingramcontent.com/pod-product-compliance
Lightning Source LLC
Chambersburg PA
CBHW070648300426
44111CB00013B/2325